T0030732

WEARING

MY

MOTHER'S

HEART

Don't neglect your mother's instruction.
What you learn from them will crown you with grace
and be a chain of honor around your neck.

Proverbs 1:8–9

Copyright © 2022 by Sophia Thakur

All rights reserved. No part of this book may be reproduced, transmitted, or stored in an
information retrieval system in any form or by any means, graphic, electronic, or mechanical,
including photocopying, taping, and recording, without prior written permission from the publisher.

First US edition 2023
First published by Walker Books (UK) 2022

Library of Congress Catalog Card Number 2022908128
ISBN 978-1-5362-3016-1

23 24 25 26 27 28 LBM 10 9 8 7 6 5 4 3 2 1

Printed in Melrose Park, IL, USA

This book was typeset in Adobe Garamond Pro.

Candlewick Press
99 Dover Street
Somerville, Massachusetts 02144

www.candlewick.com

SUSTAINABLE
FORESTRY
INITIATIVE

Certified Sourcing

www.forests.org
SFI-00854

WEARING

MY

MOTHER'S

HEART

SOPHIA THAKUR

CANDLEWICK PRESS

Introduction

My two grandmothers, while loving God, also each loved men who loved a different God. And in the Gambia, in 1965, if you were born to African, Christian fathers, you weren't expected to fall in the kind of love that swapped your father's last name for a Southeast Asian man's. My grandmothers on both sides were powerless against the pull of their hearts and chose love over tradition, boldly and publicly falling in love with men outside of their religion. To them, love should always come first, before any career. Hearing their stories carves a space for compassion in today's less forgiving society. My parents are fruit of a new seed planted in our family tree. They were born from the audacity of love.

It is rare to look at a parent and find the right example and not just the right answers. I've never known someone to dedicate themselves to love and care as much as my mum does. At least, not since her own mum, my grandmother. They keep that in common—it's a religion we are still guided by: this promise to each other.

And now, after twenty-six years of studying my mother and grandmothers, I realize that my mouth mostly speaks from the abundance of their love. While recognizing the necessity of progress, it's imperative to understand the stories that the women before us lived, to then understand why they think and reason as they do. Our experiences are vastly different.

Naturally, our opinions on love, race and womanhood clash hugely . . . but not our hearts. Our mothers' hearts we still share.

Their hearts have always been more powerful than any rule or rationale, but never more powerful than their religion. How they have worn many hearts at a time and still survived is precisely how they taught me about God. And with God, they taught me power, and with power, they opened my eyes to politics, and with politics, they showed me people . . . and from people, they gave me poetry. I hope that these poems bear that out as they lead you through reflections on family, identity, first love, grief, belief and resolution.

It took following their journeys
from Africa to London,
to understand why bravery was never a choice.
It was their only option, to survive.
I wear their hearts today, proudly . . .
Well,
at least I try

Grandma's Forbidden Love

And if all our love can ever be, is this moment,
eternity sink into a second,
pull our pulses into one.
Kiss me until the war of our histories
wraps a white flag around our tongues
and the rules of tradition
surrender to the rules of love.

All We Need Is . . .

I had someone to face life with,
and that felt like all I'd ever need
to survive the hands of this world.

Halve a Heart, Half a Life

How is it possible that you have flooded into my life
like this?
Before you, the todays and tomorrows lacked nothing,
the present was pleased, satisfied, whole, I thought.

Yet now I miss,
as if I was just delivered a heart
As if half of my brain has opened for the first time
and I am powerless but to think of how much sweeter
every tomorrow stands to be
now that I know you and know this love.

Even an Island Needs Two

For nine months, I filled my body with love
Stretched past my bones and became a home
I planted a heartbeat into the soil
Rained poems and prayers
Absorbed leaves into my bloodstream
Created a forest for you to come from
But you made a country of me,
Pushed entire seas between the plains of my skin
You taught my body to hold you
Stuffed my ears with your fingers and wrote a billion songs
to your rhythm
Wrapped me in your tablature
and we heard the world sing of how you wait
to meet us one day.

You put a new song to my ears.

I learned to listen,
to be   still

and I heard love breathe.

I untied my skin into the air
and felt your trust in every passing centimeter.

I carried the earth on my hips
Shared skin with destiny
Saw the world for what it could be
Because if sex could be this, then you are already our miracle.
We held head and hands and spoke with God about you
Asked him for your father's eyes for three hundred nights
And while mine closed, He watched over you
making room for you to become.
Cracked my life into two
One for me and one for love.

Look at how love can double us
How it reteaches us trust and time
How nine months can remind us
that union is the essence of life . . .

May we never forget

The traditions that hold
in hope of carrying us through
whatever the foreign world may put us through.

Dance—The Safe Return to Yourself

When we landed,
gold in our mouths,
our tales were cut off with our mother tongue,
but our feet were quick to refind our pulse.
So feel closely, how your body responds
to the sounds of similar souls,

and follow your rhythm back home.

If I Can No Longer Know Home, Let Me Know Heaven

We landed and our goals,
once Prophecies . . .
shrunk into only dreams.
God had never been more needed,
and so He arrived as a lifeline
that we thread through the darkness
to sew our own skyline to pray to.

If I can no longer know home,
let me know heaven.

Hope in What Cannot Be Taken from Us

2 Corinthians 4:18

What we learned quickly is
how unimpressed heaven is
by what seduces our senses.
Suddenly, with nothing,
it became everything to remember
only expensive souls
can buy Eternity.

So we grew rich, naked, while wearing everything we had
and watching it grow into everything we could afford to need.

Our hope, our fortress, our God in whom we trust.

Psalm 62:5

It Was a Different Time

We had an understanding
that some things must be done
in the absence of desire.
In a culture of scales
that tip to tradition,
my sisters and I grate our fingertips
away in the kitchen,
callous to our kaleidoscope dreams,
blink into the eyes of society,
stand behind the mirror
and hold our hips.

We read them in Braille . . .

"You are function before you are female."

Wooden Jewelry

Grandmother's story
is wildly unsettling.
Not because of what I know,
and has weaved her strength into our souls,
but because of what isn't discussed over dinners
but still eats at the bliss in her eyes.

What happened to you
that you should be so brave?
That you surrendered to such faith
as if it's all you had
that couldn't be taken.

God was more
than your parents' lesson to you as a little girl.
The altar was the only place you trusted to look
while your back was turned to the world.

What made you command the spirit of your children into
the Lord's hands
before your own?

Who abused their power?
Who tried to steal your gold?

Wearing Our Mothers

My Grandma's smile was
a pebble landing into the satin sheet of a lake
opening the sun into ten million little waves
reflecting back onto any face
lucky enough to experience her light,
her raise.
Never ever ever in vain, in our veins.

Silent Woman, Silent World

Till you build a country on your hips
to multiply what lives
and give your body into the unknown
for a whole life to break in
and turn your skeleton to a gallery,
a museum of creation . . .

Till you have worn grace like the ocean wears a wave
and clawed strength from the scared
to embolden their bravery . . .
Till you have observed the world
and trained your mouth in such a way
to pack whole universes into the few things you're permitted
to say . . .

Till you have stood in the storm
and pulled from it a Nile,
spun water from a desert
and turned bricks to a home
you cannot question the power
that a woman, a mother, holds.

We taught all of humanity how skin could come alive in the
womb,
through touch, in the bedroom

we rise up a people
who carry our breath on their lips.

A woman has always been
what it means to live.

Grandmother of the Land

Remember me fondly
for how I felt wrapped around the palms of your
adolescence.
For the pulse in my fingertips
that learned your rhythm,
your language,
just to teach it back to your children,
who would come back as their reflection
after some years
and treat us as fools.

Remember me kindly
for how I gave up my tongue for you
and hoaxed my blood to forget,
to make space to learn your ways
and brand your culture into my neck.

Remember me graciously
for how I would lower my head as you walk
down the aisle to marry your power.
Us, throwing our rice for your feet.
Us, throwing salt behind our heads.

Remember me wise.
Remember me mute.
But mostly,

Remember me a mother
to this country and his yutes,
because my seed will not forget
what you did to their roots.

Hall Party

Hackney in the early 2000s,
Gambian benachin* filling the wind,
musorr** and chins to the sky.
Open toes for the win.

Davido and D'banj,
Youssou N'Dour and 2face,
we join our old choir
in this new new place.

Parking at the hall party
Three kisses while holding pots
Food warmers holding our mothers.
Our bodies never forgot the cloth
that wraps home to home
and home to heart.

Hide it all, keep it ours.

*jollof
**head wraps

Icarus Servicing Britain

Britain, eagle of the west
Wings woven by women
Who crushed garlic into ghee
And gave the streets curry and biryani, and kebab.

Britain, eagle of the west
Claws sharpened by men
Migrants
Who hoped the bricks they laid
could build a home for them too.

Britain, eagle of the west
Feathers of foreigners
ignorant to what makes you fly.

City of Stolen Souls

A statue collects stares
from eyes that assume
something of them was so good,
so honorable
that to only immortalize them in the mind
was not enough.
To read the plaque is rare—
to search the name is rare.
Our great assumptions are cemented in the pride of a statue.

So they stand,
mysteries memorialized,
great grains of granite gathered
into lips that led sons to war.
Carefully arranged stone
to mold eyes that saw
and bought
Slaves.
Men who strove to walk an entire race
to its grave.

Oh, how this city still celebrates
how our streets still commemorate crime.
By plating the past in gold
and parading it across the eyes
of migrants who were torn from their very homes

by this very man.
This very chapter in history
that they say has been stripped of its honor
yet still these trophies stand
Golden Grim Reapers.

If these are lessons that we take pride in having learned
pull down the decorations
let the balloons be burst
and let death come to all that we insist has died.

But If the Statues Must Stay . . .

Dedicate us at least a bench
Somewhere to rest the legs
of the two hundred and twenty thousand
non-white staff members of the NHS
who were hardly allowed a second to sit
throughout every war and Covid.

Plant us at least a tree
to remember the three hundred and eighty thousand
Black soldiers
who ensured England could breathe—
in their foreign and final breath
as their funeral but Britain's victory.

At least a plaque or a wreath
for the minority majority of the high street
that has always upheld this economy.

Immortalize the sacrifice
not the one holding the knife.
To what we still give glory, history makes right.

Science to My Mother's Silence

Cognitive rewiring suggests
that history is carried
in the very DNA of our breath
the silent frequencies of trauma
tucked away in our great-great-grandchildren's heads
old, buried anxieties of the brain
born decades ahead of the heart.

If Grandma's voice was taken
I will find it somewhere in my heart.

Heartbreak's Continuum

I wonder if it breaks our elders' hearts
to see us riot, and petition and march
for the same things they left Africa to gain . . .
fair opportunity, better living, better education.

I wonder what happens at the window of their minds
as we put their legs back on the street,
wear their mouths to repeat the haunted poetry
of failed freedom.

I wonder if the nostalgia hurts
or gives way to guilt or rage
I wonder how heavy it might be
carrying kids who're carrying your weight.

Grandma's Interlude

Toni Morrison wrote about Martin Luther King Jr. that he made the most important things to him irresistible to others. What a legacy to leave . . . making the responsibility to help others so attractive, so habitual.

A parent may always see their child as finer than they are. Incapable of abandoning their moral compass, even at the hands of such a different world. A grandparent, even more so. I uphold the same audacious faith in my grandchildren's capacity that I did years back, marching on the streets of West London, for change to come.

For what we have begun, I am helplessly hopeful that my children will finish. We gave them a world with plenty of holes in the dam. We wade and we wait for them to break into and dismantle the ocean. To pull the bloody carpet from the water's floor and drown the old ways.

I trust them to reimagine. To organize. To rebel against the imposed limits of their race, and rise up a nation that celebrates the end of an empire
although built on our backs, paid fully in blood.
By hands of my hands,
change must surely come.

The Best Perspectives

If you are going to see yourself
through anyone's eyes, let it be God's
next, *let it be your mother's . . .*

Just Enough Change

Hope is essential to helplessness
to inspire our knees from the ground
to march.
We are powerless but to be faithful
that this too shall pass.
But nobody told me,
and it was blissful to never ask
how hope and helplessness
throughout history have shared the same dance.
In and out of each other's arms
till we move between them both
in a blinding, hopeful trance.

If the people are kept dancing long enough
the rhythm begins to feel as though it comes from within
and just like that, we are mistaken to think that
the white world also sings
to the melody of our skin . . .
And there's *just enough* progress
And *just enough* conversation about change
to keep our dancing feet moving and shaking.
While the real war takes a seat
in the corner of the dance
waiting for the music to stop
and we realize the chants
just echo and bounce between the chambers of our mouths

Against the wall of white lips
right back into our own Black ears.
It's not change we hear, it's our hope.

Do not be alarmed,
Black child,
When the veil is torn down
and you are told it is safe to take off your armor
and the heads of helplessness and hope turn around
carrying the same face of their white father.

The system is not ours,
we are just played in as dancers.

Reimagine a Revolution

The pessimist knows only defeat
like a foreshadow cast over his life,
but failure is only as final
as those unwilling to try.
Although winter revolves around us,
summer is not dead.
It has not been defeated,
the change is not the end.
When a leaf falls in autumn
no tree will say it has failed.
Defeat is less a destination
than it is a part of the trail.

Guncotton

In India the first film stock was made
with the same compound found in explosives.
Art and its power to uproot our lives
had never become quite the metaphor.
The conflict between the people's voice and the dictatorship
danced together on their tiptoes,
on a big screen
in a minefield.

In 1897 in Paris a fire started at a film screening.
One hundred twenty-six people's lives were radicalized
at the hands of art.

The compound used in the film was later banned,
and then also began
the banning of stories that stood to be just as explosive
in a silenced society.

The compound was called guncotton.

Harmless or deadly
The question to which all censorship responds.

There is a lot that I miss
but nothing as much as who I used to be
before I was forced to be who I had to be.

Fatherhood

How you found fatherhood in your future
after a fatherless past.
How you lived with holes in your heart
but still took such a chance
to fill them with more blood, more family,
with more prayers and more bandages than vanishings.
How you wrapped our mishandlings in the forgiveness
that I'm not even sure you've extended to your youth.
We recognize and give thanks
to the God so evident in you.

Daddies and Daughters

I never knew how quickly fear doubles, in love
How your worries could also steal the sleep from my nights
If I could, I'd slip your heart
from beneath your skin
And have it sleep in my palms tonight.

Patriotic to the Past

When I was a little girl in the pews
and my parents would come back from drinking the blood
they looked like a Mafia couple,
Halos heavy with how much the altar should hopefully
never know of their hearts.
My dad, moving in slow motion,
carrying the weight of some crosses and some sins from the
country he left.
But still, they walked down the aisle like newlyweds every
Sunday.
My mum held his arm like a flag to a pole,
patriotic to a person.
From those pews I fell in love with the nobility of tradition
alone
and prayed one day, for such an allegiance to a feeling,
bold enough to parade it before God.

Dad & Mum

They came from broken homes,
promised a broken home wouldn't come from them.
Even when backs were turned on each other
they at least turned in the same bed.
Even when they met the seam that split both of their
parents
they held tight to the promise of their new threads.
My parents,
the first of their kind . . .
Lovers that try
and are honored by time.

Pied Piper

My mum pulls her twist back,
water slides behind the shore.
The world watches the sand of her shoulders
gather and pinch together behind her hair
by her mother's fingers.
How a lady should stand
etched into Mum's skin like
the Afro on the hairline of the wave.

She pulls the breath from anybody
who has seen her pull the tide back.
Like God blowing the night
from the way of the sun.

Say

Do not apologize
for what your Mother and I
have spent years hoping you would do.

Your mouth is an altar
that we have prepared for you,
so come
from behind the shadow of your tongue
to stand inside your mouth
And Speak.

Reigning Proverbs

Whichever campfire lived inside the stories of my Grandma
shared its flame with my mother's griot lips
The same fire, both candle and blowtorch.
The delicateness. Sometimes flower, sometimes bomb
Words like water, for wounds or for war.
I wear the mouths of women who parted their lips like a sea
And journeyed men into martyrs for their families.
Kisses coating them with new honey,
filling valley'd hearts into hills of homes.

The women before me would loosen their tongues
To rain proverbs and poems over us,
To pull the shadows back behind people who ran from the sun,
To turn them to face what they stood to become
if they should dare to dance in their own light.
Dare to give gravity their jaw,
unpin their tongue and give sound to the Braille of their bodies.

My lips vibrate in the joining of mouths,
My grandmother's to my own,
through strength remembered
and stories retold.

Observe

I'm sure the wind around her froze
as her uncle, my brother, showed his age.
I know my daughter well,
her skin became a cage.
A bottle with an ocean stuffed in it.
Shaken.
I wondered in that moment
if her father and I had made a mistake
in encouraging her to always unscrew her lips,
to always speak.
Knowing the tsunamis she keeps under ice,
we still trained her in her fire.

So there she sits,
evidence of our parenting.
Eyes fixed
Bottom lip bit
Weighing up whether to speak and let rip,
or ideally for me, remember that sometimes silence is also
speech,
just this once until her uncle leaves.

There's something about moments like this
Seconds before jumping off a cliff
Seconds before a first kiss
Seconds before you give a mouth
to what's been brewing between your ribs

Seconds of stillness
where what sits in your vision is the only thing to exist.
She became a postcard
Her face, a desert
Us, alchemists.
Journeying
past forehead, cheeks
to recognize our flag, hanging from her lips.
We wait for the decision of the wind
Whose lips today?

We have both taken turns speaking from them.

When she is in love, mine
When she has had enough, His
Poetic, piercing, unkissed.

And as she drew them apart like a sun
tearing through a timid sky
the room became as silent as eyes fixed on the horizon.
I wondered whether today
her mouth was a flower or grenade.
Whether from the floors of her jaw
she would pick up and piece power with grace,
And bloom . . .
Or turn her mouth into a minefield
and strike her uncle's opinion up the dry spine of her throat.

No one survives the latter,
maybe not even her.

Attempt—Grandma

We didn't have what you have today, baby. There were no stages
for our confidence.
We had men who shared custody of our lips.
Who obligated themselves to managing our limbs, our freedom.
But you . . . Your voice is yours. Ours.
Heavy with everything we wish we could've said.
Wish we could've screamed from the streets
with cardboard signs over our heads demanding more.
We dreamt of women like you living somewhere in the garden.
Somewhere in the branches of our family tree
would arrive a woman prepared to burn down the village just to
be free.

Your uncle spoke over you on Sunday.
Tumbled some dated ideas into a conversation about
womanhood.
Your mum and my heads, under history's hands, sunk as he spoke
about women needing to focus on the home, and leave feminism
alone.
But somewhere in the room, all the wind gathered to raise your
chin.
I looked up and over to where the sweet sound of softening
rocks was coming from
and of course it was coming from you.
From the things we have told you in private
From the Toni Morrison essays shaking inside of you
From the dust of men you've gathered in your pens

From a voice that has never had to surrender,
you questioned the root of his thinking,
but without insult and without judgment.

This part of your tongue is from us,
the ocean honoring the lake.
You spoke a bridge between everyone in the room.
You let my old palms guide you to his entry point,
which opens to that which is softly spoken.
He paused and let the recent years simmer into his clock,
and smiled distantly at how times have changed.
I watched calendars have a conversation,
about what from the old still stands to work.
Your uncle believes in a balance that no longer serves
women who like to work.
Who have to work.
Women whose wombs are filled with both babies and businesses.
Your uncle is not wrong for liking things the old way,
if in his years, in his ears, that way worked best.
That seems to be something you kids forget,
that not everyone must want or believe the same thing.
Just because you cannot morally oblige,
does not make it objectively anything.

Even with such certainty crashing waves behind your cheeks,
you threw him questions instead of disagreeing.

You have your mother's grace,
and none of my restraint

Thank God.

A Mouth Full of Joy

Qu'il vienne, qu'il vienne
a time when joy astounds us
and floods through the pockets of our teeth
pushing sadness far away from the shore.
Qu'il vienne, qu'il vienne
laughter that roars
the elderly into believing
that maybe there is more
than a life half-lived
Half-loved
Half-seen.

May it come, may it come
joy that softens the callus
and pulls rest in for the blessed
and pulls closed that past chapter
and finally speaks on something else.

Temporary Elation

Untie your Afro
Untie your fist
Bring down your arms
With the banner in it
Put down your microphone
Untweet your tweets
Turn off the news
Empty the streets
Pull back from the conversation
Delete that email to HR
Stop attending D&I
Wait right where you are
With your eyes forward
And your skin black
And for a moment
Do just that
You have been in a civil war
With your skin, for how long?
Trying to convince how much of the world
That you deserve rights
And you belong?
Do you even remember what it's like?
Skin removed from the fight?
Tip your neck back
Face the sun
Afford yourself a moment
for all that has been pressed into you
to become undone.

The beginning of love is the beginning of everything.

When We Meet in Paris

When we meet in Paris
bump into me at the bar.
Hold eye contact for a second too long,
stare as I depart.
Indulge in my glance over a shoulder,
meet my face with a smile.
Slightly raise your glass to me,
a toast to our brief denial.
My chin will turn back to where I'm walking
with a grin that recognizes a spark.
I'll drink wine with my sisters
move our hips an inch too far, too fast . . .
twirl away from the arms of my ladies
and catch your eye from the corner afar.
You'll stand like a man in the crowd
with a golden ticket to my heart.
You'll pull closer as if by a rope
and the water between us will part.
A beeline to my dress line,
you hold my hip
and open your palm,
and there, in the night of Paris,
we begin our first and forever dance.

Daydream

My eyes have found new joy
since you began
flowing through them like the softest daydream.
Now, they love to wake almost as much
as they loved to dream of you

before you came and connected the two.

Blindfolded

(read after listening to Jhené Aiko's "You Are Here")

Somehow, while only meeting at the odd eclipse,
the moon and sun find a way to live
in trust of each other,
submitting themselves entirely,
hopeful, prideless.

I pray that you are who I think you are,
a man with his eyes on only one.
I pray I can trust you to be the moon
during the setting of my sun.
In my absence,
I pray you stay present in our love.

If God Is Love . . .

If love is God, of course
our bodies reject romance when lukewarm
and half-baked gestures
and the withholding of tenderness.

If it truly is a gift,
a piece of God Himself in us all . . .
may we welcome it, full.
Learning love's alchemy
of pride into pleasure
and fear into full faith
that being giving of our love
will never leave an empty space.

The ocean has always opened to the rivers of the land,
fearlessly, generously,
extending its hand

And look at how powerful that makes its force,
connecting the entire world
back to the source.

Romance

Love me
Twelve roses
for the twelve days leading up to the date of our first kiss
Love me in a playlist of songs that we sing together
Love me in handwritten notes with French quotes
tucked into the pockets of my coats
to be found and translated once I'm home
Love me in poems . . .
in places that are almost as beautiful
as you say I am to you
Love me in food,
in trying something new
just so that it is ours.
Love me in "I'd love to see you in this dress tonight"
Love me in surprise
Love me loud
Love me like I own your eyes in any crowd
Love me in the dance
when my day has been too rough for words
Love me in knowledge of where to kiss when it hurts
Pull up
to pray
to cover my day
with faith and takeaway
with flowers and Lucozade
for long drives
to listen to new albums.

Love me in the possessive
in the obsessive and the restless
Kiss me till I'm breathless
Miss me when I'm resting
Insist on love
till we see God
in everything born between us.

Heartburn

It felt like we never needed matches,
or the sun.
A throbbing glow of what was shared between us
lit every candle in the world.
Our love burned
like we were born entirely of gasoline,
stuffed with perfume,

kissing with mouths of fire.

Heartache, Heartspace

I create distance,
try to train my mind a new angle
but that space,
how quickly it fills with everything I miss.
How easy it is, to love you again
from outside the frame, I try to forget . . .

But all this heart will do is remember.

Friendship Breakup

Where have you gone
with my laughter

Where have you gone
with my love

Where have you gone
with my secrets

Where have you gone
with my trust?

Friendzone

I tied my heart around a lamppost
to light up your walk home

I squeezed it into your phone screen
to call when you're alone

I tucked my heart into your pocket
for you to hold when you are nervous

I hid it in a photo album
to find accidentally on purpose

I flattened it into the mirror
in hope you'd love your reflection a little more

I wrapped it around your laces
to give you more support

I slid it between your laugh
to hopefully share the joke with

I pressed it onto your eyelids
so here's to hoping

that you wake up and see
that the safest place to leave your heart
has always been right here, with me.

Trifling

I wish every part of me stayed new to you.
Maybe this is why people leave,
to go and be adored and seen
for the first time again.

Feeling Right

Was building a home in your arms
Was giving my secrets over to you,
to cancel out my solitude.
It was telling my family that I had met a man
who I would love to raise a family with.
It was learning love as told by your lips.
It was counting the days
by when I'd next see your face
and the hours by when we last spoke.
It was giving so many of my years to you
in love, in trust, in hope
that forever was ours to hold
for as long as we lived and loved.

It felt so right to mold my life
around my favorite thing in it.
But now, alone,
I walk around myself, wondering,

Where all of me has gone?

Trust Issues

I would love to trust another with my heart
but it's still too sensitive to touch new palms.
Too fresh a worry, a wound,
another woman.

Riskier Nostalgia

It has been so easy to refuse to give
my heart unto something new.
But still not as easy as giving my heart
right back to you.

Toxic Battle

You're the piece of the past I keep coming back to . . .
A lesson I keep forgetting I've learned,
that when either of these cages opens
even slightly
it unleashes the kind of love that eventually hurts.
But still . . .
let me lay
in the arms of this carcass
that we stuffed with just enough of us
to survive one more love
one more kiss
one more breath
to tear from each other . . .

and see who chokes first.

Give Me Back Myself

I did everything right
but at the peak
you stepped over my summit
to see something of the sea . . .
You climbed me,
felt the power in your limbs
and decided to see how far you could swim.

So now I rip oceans apart within me,
to look for her.
I climb down the steps of myself,
to drown in search of what might've been worth
your attention.
I soak in the shores of your rejection
Wear your eyes in my reflection
While scraping away at my carcass.

Hungry
I run to you
to give me my name back.
To replace this pain with
at least admittance of your mistake.
To give my smile back to my face.
But I am met
with a sharper arrow than the last.

For me, time has romanticized hope.
For you, it has fixed me to your past.
But still, I wait at the window,
cheeks pushed blue and pink against the glass
for you to adopt my broken pieces
and put home back in me.
But you are derelict of us.

The end of love can feel
like the end of everything.

There is no heart big enough
to house both the memories and the grief.
We must speak.

Not Enough

I cannot believe that all you can ever be to me now
is a memory.
You do not fit into just a thought.

You spill from my eyes some nights.
My heart leaks through the floor.

Gap in the Air

You were an empty seat at my wedding.
A silent speech at the reception.
A tearless face during my first dance.
An empty palm during labor.
You were clapping hands that never touched,
when baby took his first steps.
A gap in the air on Bonfire Night.
An uneaten plate at Christmas.
Silence on the other side of the phone
as I call you for the seventh time this week
and hold my breath as your answering machine
pierces your voice through my heart.

And again, I tell you all about my day
imagining the things you'd say.

Letting Death Come to the Dying

I must relearn you
Meet you again for the first time
Allow you to reintroduce yourself
As a thought, this time,
as a memory.
As a friend I cannot hold
but hear.
So copy the wind for me
Or the sun
For its distance, but a presence
that is never undone.

I watch you become a candle
in the attic of my mind.
Never blown out, never goodbye . . .
For He wraps our future together in eternity.
And I'll wear your memory until we both return to Him.

Death is never our end . . .

Sing After Listening to Joel Baker's "Hope Sweet Hope"

Let's pretend the soil, is just a duvet
Tucking the memories, into a new day
and every sunrise, is lifted with your eyes
The seasons are seconds, life is on your time

Who told the ending
It wasn't forever?
You're still alive to me
Dancing in heaven

Spring in Ends

A sharp air, sure of the morning it brings
to the window of his.
Crisp.
The wind wanders around waiting
For people to dance between . . .
And from the window, with stolen time
he watches the pharmacist unfold herself from sleep
and the mother unsew herself from her kid
as she picks up some space from the school gate.
He lets the tree beneath him
happen again and again in his eyes,
scans the branches into his memory
and Spring, he archives.
Today, blossoms blush
on the fingertips of bark,
like a palm, opening to behold a new season.
The people below can feel it
The baker with his back to the shop shutters
presses his hands to his hips, breathes in and smiles satisfied . . .
Winter has finally passed.
Three blue jays sing to a handful of blossom
on the tree that was a desert just yesterday.
The wind dances to their song.
The morning sun turns and twists
into every window that had been waiting to taste it.
But from his window

there's just something about those blue jays
that freezes the frame and makes a postcard of a place.
They chose here. Nobody ever chooses here.

Here, they aren't really birds . . .
Not here.
Those aren't the kind of birds that sing here.
Not like how the siren swings its voice through the knuckles
of concrete.
Like a spirit after its son.

The block in spring
will have you imagining
how beautiful blossoms must be in a town
that has the time to look up.

It's a blue plastic bag
that just couldn't untangle itself
from the window.
They watch each other like cell mates.

Author's note:

Grenfell Tower was a twenty-four-story apartment block housing some of the most unlucky residents in London. The building material used to build these apartments was highly flammable. In fear of death, the residents complained, but they were ignored. From their windows, they overlooked the most expensive part of London, where any cracks in the pavements were filled by morning. And where the blue jays gathered in their nest on June 14, 2017, to discuss where all of that smoke was coming from.

If only the residents in Grenfell Tower were birds. If only the council had listened,

or built more than one way down.

Strong Surrender

The men in my life are rarely permitted to feel,
until it breaks them,
to let it in, until it impossibly hurts.
As if ignoring an open wound
could make things anything but worse.
But the world has taught their body
to stretch scars into smiles
and wedge miles between their mind and mouth.
His tongue was foreign to speaking about it.
Suicide was how he shouted.

I Need You to Crumble

If your head would just deflate
through the burn holes in your thoughts

If your eyelids would just lie there wet,
washed up on shore

If your neck would untense
and hang like a flag with no wind

And your shoulders
surrender to

gravity

If your back would only bend
and almost break under the pressure

And your knees almost snap out of place
under the weight

If your ankles would only crumple
like a can being crushed

Perhaps then the world will wake
to the load men do not talk about
but carry throughout each day.

Sleep On It

Wellness was waiting for things to pass
or settle like butter used to the heat.

Mental illness was an accent we were never told we had.
One we would sink into like a well
and drown in,
thinking that life was just a beach.

My parents had to decide which matters could be given medals
to raise to the pedestal of a mouth.

What's gotten dire enough to be okay to talk about
out loud?

We copy our heroes. Their strength and their silence.

So I also found ways to swallow everything
that couldn't shine if it were to hang from my neck.

Fertile after the Fire

Too soft
They say
Too sensitive
Too easy for kids these days

But isn't this what you were working for?
Isn't this what you hoped would change?

Bridging the Gaps between Me

Tomorrow is already better
because today I took the first step
You asked and I finally said
that there is a war happening in my head

Yesterday was the last of tomorrows
that I have to get through alone
I said I feel trapped away by my thoughts
and you built a bridge for me to come home.

Doing It Broken Is Part of Doing It

You'll be all right
The sun may shatter, but it still shines

Winning Side

You can . . .
Even while it's still sad
Still fresh
Still confusing
You can move on
Even though it's hard.

The lessons
The overcoming you've had to do
The toughest days you've seen through
The strength that you had to pull
It's all still with you!
You're the reason your tears dried!
Look at what you are made of!
Look at all of you on your side!

Reframing

Why use wonder to worry
when you could use it to wish and believe
Why use creativity to doubt
when you could instead use it to dream
Why use vision to set boundaries
when you should be using it to see,
everything that's waiting
for you to achieve.

In Jesus's Image

Made by Christ's hands who put a candle in the sky
to remind us that we can still glow
in the peak of the night.

Mama's Outro—Everyone Has Beauty

The most beautiful people I have ever met have taken my breath away not with anything on their skin, but with who they decide to be everyday. If there's one thing time has taught me, it's that beauty looks less and less like a face, and more like a feeling. It's the peace you carry in your personality. It's how you commit yourself to kindness and integrity. Beauty is a grateful heart. It's consistency and communication. Beauty is hanging up your ego before stepping into resolution. It's waking up everyday and trying to be the right version of yourself. It's in the moments you just have to stare at someone in awe, of how similar their heart must be to God. This is the true and most important measure of beauty.

Nine Months Certain

If only for a moment
I could borrow my mother's eyes
and see myself as she does,
love myself as she does,
believe in myself with the same certainty she does,
as if all I can do is prosper.

I guess after carrying me for nine months,
she is well trained in the faith
that whenever there is cause to push
only in complete surrender to bravery
can you deliver on what you were born to do.

That Compliment Is Yours

Let yourself be kissed
Open your lips
Swallow the good that they say about you
Open your limbs, make space
for those compliments to take their rightful place.

Thank You, Body

I sat on the edge of the earth
Legs waterfalling from the ledge
Arms as pillars balancing the weight of my head,
I inhaled the entire sky into my shoulders
And thanked every part of my body
for remaining mine
even when I denied my pride in it.

Make My Mirror Great Again

We should be content
to look at other lives,
other women's limbs
men's money and other women's eyes
as things that are not comments
on our own personal lives

So

Claim your eyes back
Claim your thighs back
Your body is built for more than change
Your nose is perfect
So are your lips
Your side profile
And your frame
Your eyes are the perfect shape for you
Your skin the perfect shade
You are personally perfect
Exactly as you were made.

Grandma's Outro—You Dey Craze

One day you will come to feel how similar a girl is to God.
Perhaps into a small boy's ear, a temple will push itself
through your teeth and as if possessed he will denounce his
mouthguard and decide his denomination is whatever will
have him ascend you like a rope. Or a prayer.

Worship will follow you in whistles as you walk. And one
day a man will baptize his story, pull himself from his past
like a grape and press it under bended knees until he leaks
empty, and he will, from the earth, ask you to be his finest
garden to tend to. He will offer you his eternity in exchange
for your name. And all I can hope is that by this hour your
lineage would have lifted from your bones to mix into your
blood like clay so that even as he brands you with diamonds,
with a foreign finish to the name your mother sealed you
with . . . your finger will still feel like your father's. Slightly
bent into a bow knuckle, and ready to remember if ever a
man should have you forget that you are fruit from gardens
of trees before him. Your seed is already seasoned.

In all your glory, all that Grandma asks
is that you remember
God was God before man was made.
And God saw you and was pleased
Before Adam's gaze.
You do not need a man
to feel like a lady

But oh, baby . . .

Your hips will fill and find fingers to contain the age that vibrates your body into craving. With cheeks full of cherries and eyes glazed, you will trade out your dolls for your reflection. Comb your own hair. Pinch the small of your own dress in search of shapes like sand dunes. Your dressing table will become an altar like your mother's before you. You'll hold your breath to find Atlantis. Reason to be kissed without coming up for air. A new world of women to discover when you put the dolls down, and play with your reflection. I hope. Oh, I pray that you look upon her fondly. Because we were beautiful before anybody had to say so . . . and you look just like us. And I hope that, in the age of other women, other filters and makeup products, you can still love the canvas you came from.

Your mother's face is heavy with history. When she was your age it sat like an atlas on her neck and men would wander it looking for treasure at the end of an open trail. In the city she grew up in, husbands still walk around looking for their wives . . . looking for your mother. They walk in circles, from their workplaces to their marriage beds, wondering how far Atlantis is. How far your mother moved. How far their hands could go before they were smacked away by the father that lived at the wrist of the good women of the city. My husband, waiting at the door ten minutes before curfew for your mother to come home, the gatekeeper to her integrity.

The King of her name.

He says your mother has let you become wild.
He doesn't understand you've been unchained
From shackles of shame-filled pride.
Of tradition that insists on keeping all of a woman inside
Her voice
Her thoughts
What her body can become on a dance floor.
You, grandbaby,
Are all of the women that came before
That simply couldn't . . .
So do
If not for us
For you
Let everything in you seep through
I hope to catch a glimpse, if only a droplet . . . of what I
would've been like if born to your time. And I'm sure that's
the reason behind your mother's slow smile.
You're wild . . . and oh
how we wish we were.

Self-Love Is the Best Love

I vow to never abandon my peace
for a piece of the past that didn't last
I vow to give my future
a more confident and happy heart
I vow to never depart from my joy
For the sake of takers and fakers
Or leave my cup vacant
while filling the cups of strangers
I vow to stay close to my sanity
and tear myself from comparison
I vow to embrace my reality
and trust God will manage things
I vow to always remember
And never forget
God gave the tools for my painting
I am my own to make and take
I am the artist of my fate.

Oh, Brothers

In a world more worried about what a woman wears
than the reasons most women find themselves scared
to walk home in the dark
or alone in the park
or into a meeting full of men
I'm sure my father gives thanks
for my brothers

My pillars
My princes
My armor in incident
My lighthouses
and words of wisdom
My seat in the storm
and strength to pull through
My reminder of the title we are called too
Thakur,
Nobility,
Brave.
My brothers make me feel blessed
to share this very name.

Finding God

You have reminded me
how much of myself I find
in the company of those who chose to love me
time after time after time

Acknowledgments

Even if I scrubbed my heart with every lemon in the world,
I'm still not sure it would be as clean as my mother's. Thank
you, Mama, for being so much better than you even realize.
I wouldn't be half the woman I am today if it weren't for
your unwavering, powerful, powerful love. I wish everyone
whose life is made better by you simply being a part of it
realized this and honored you accordingly. But your soft,
stained-on smile reminds me that you know where your
rewards are stored. Waiting on the other side of those
golden gates. Dad, Latir, Jai . . . thank you for teaching me
that a man can be both strong and unspeakably sensitive.
Remembering your lessons has saved me more times than
you'll ever know. Nanny, Grandma, Aunty Simone, Aunty
Maria and Aunty Chinelo . . . thank you for so willingly
being evidence of God. Evidence of how love's activism can
bloom entire gardens across the world. You are some of the
greatest women I've ever known. Thank you to everyone
who has become a sister to me over the years. It's a blessing
to not have to look further than the family to see God's
best work.

And finally, a huge thank you to my team. Lynsey, Abigail:
thank you, both, for believing in me so much more than
I often believe in myself. Sometimes I survive solely off of
your confidence in me. I don't know what this collection
would have been without you both. Thank you, Justin
and Kim, for teaching me how to put poetry first, and let

the world meet me there. And, Jane . . . you were the first person who had me imagine that maybe I could be an author.

There aren't enough thank-yous in the world for taking my hand and guiding me into my purpose.

God bless you all, abundantly.

Find out more at
www.sophiathakur.co.uk